In *All the Lands We Inherit*, Darby Price's contemporary recasting of the biblical book, Lamentations, the author offers us a book of hybridity, uneasy with the confines and conventions of a single genre. She weaves lyric to narrative, affliction and misery to compassion and filial love.

One might read this book as a sequence of prose poems—compact, bristling with image and insight—or perhaps as a book of prose, novel-like in its complexities, memoir-like as it seeks to unknot the entanglement of memory, while avoiding the easy conclusions of a memorial.

At the center of Price's meditation is the figure of the mother, her mother—a lively, complicated, righteous, and stubborn person—for whom the book is a pre-elegy, a lament that is at times harrowing and at times humorous, a portrait that is at times tender with, at times confounded with, its subject. Across the book's sixty-six lyric vignettes, Price confronts the burden and blessing that is her mother, a body on its journey from the womb to the grave, a presence that foretells an absence, a severance that calls for lamentation.

—ERIC PANKEY, author of *The History of the Siege*

ALL THE LANDS WE INHERIT

ALL THE LANDS WE INHERIT

DARBY PRICE

BLACK LAWRENCE PRESS

Black Lawrence Press

Executive Editor: Diane Goettel
Cover and Interior Design: Zoe Norvell
Cover Artwork: "Scent of Broq-pa 12052020" by Ziesook You

Copyright © Darby Price
2025

ISBN: 978-1-62557-1-601

All rights reserved. Except for brief quotations in critical articles or reviews, no part of this book may be reproduced in any manner without prior written permission from the publisher: editors@blacklawrencepress.com

Published 2025 by Black Lawrence Press.
Printed in the United States.

for Cory Jean

CONTENTS

1
All the Lands We Inherit: A Lament

69
Acknowledgements

71
References

Remembering mine affliction and my misery,
the wormwood and the gall.
My soul hath them still in remembrance,
and is humbled in me.
This I recall to my mind, therefore have I hope.

Lamentations 3:18-20

All of the years gone by, siphoned off by the usual things: bills and schedules and our own lives taking root, taking up space. My mother sits in a worn chair next to her hospital bed. Beside her, the compressor gurgles, churning out oxygen for her weakened lungs. *Maybe I'm here to redefine what can be done*, she says, with a note of challenge in her voice. She's been taking steroids, and this has given her greater physical energy and more emotional zip than she's had in years. The zip, like everything else, must be managed. I tell her again and again that she cannot be an Uber driver because she doesn't have a car. Cannot pay for cabs to the grocery store if she doesn't have a job. And cannot make six figures blogging, no matter what the lady in the room down the hall might have told her. My mother does not like my booming voice. I am an angel skirting the borders of her hope, fearful and full of light. My mother hides her face.

Anger is a poison, but so are the narratives we weave for the sake of the people we love. Stories like a sleep mask laid gently over the eyes. A calming dark. If you cannot see the parameters of the room, or the black widow scaling the wall, you cannot lose a wink. Nevermind the smoke creeping in through the jamb. Nevermind the creature in the back of the closet. Behind the soft black silk, a room we create for ourselves.

Anything we say can and will be held against us. My sister returns to the hotel where I sit in an abandoned conference room, working on Medicaid applications. *She says that I've been ripping her heart to shreds all week,* she says as she falls into a chair. The fluorescent light makes crags between her eyebrows. I offer her Scotch in a coffee mug. She accepts, and reads excerpts from a medical report she pulls from her bag: *evidence of ischemic attacks.* Pulmonary hypertension. And, of course, emphysema. The smoke that curled from my mother's hand was always a distinguishing mark—that, and a dachshund now so old he's gone deaf and is weakened by cancer. *Always the practical one,* my mother will sneer when I tell her the dog should be euthanized. *I could have wished for more compassion.* And the years stretch out behind and before me, full of shame and terror. I know what happened here. I know more than my mother would want me to say. I want to say everything, to lay bare what we often demand from mercy. To be, as Hawthorne says, true about my worst. To lay this burden down.

Build me a sand castle and fill it with wine, she used to say. *Leave me at the water's edge at low tide.* Then, the other day: *If you hear that I died alone in my apartment, just know that I wasn't unhappy.* A grim end preferable to paper cups full of pills, sponge baths from strangers, a time-table lunch every day. A hallway full of folks like her with walkers and wheelchairs and bodies that smell of astringent. *Just send me off on an ice floe,* she jokes. Or, more seriously: *Jesus could come for me still.*

Blue: the tint in my mother's palms. Cool note against the heat of a long and baleful spring. The color of my grief, which darkens when I study it. It shifts shape. Now it is a sleeping bird. Now, a long and hollow boat. Now, the edge of a map that no one has yet traversed.

Birthright not as lands and blessings, but the inheritance we cannot avoid. My trust is the stubbornness of a great-grandmother whose tuberculosis shortened her leg, and who rowed herself to work each day before marriage and children put an end to all that. The sensitivities of a grandmother who was kind and addicted to drink. And not above all, but clearly, the impulsivity of a mother who is like a buoy unmoored, still afloat but wildly adrift. It was she who taught me, *If you're sitting in the pew and something doesn't sound right, go to the source and read it yourself.* The memory of bouncing on her hip as she danced across the living room. *One, two-three-four-five,* she sang, taking four rhythmic steps forward. I squealed with delight. *Mighty Tigers don't take no jive!* Four steps back. A cheer routine my sister had learned. *Six, seven-eight-nine-ten!* she sang as I clung to her, thin arms wrapped around her neck. *Back it up and do it again!* My mother and I move forward. We move back. The hip, the neck, the dance. The song in the throat and the child begging *Again.*

Could have been anything: wood carver, sommelier, model, college graduate. Could have joined the throngs of women who wanted to smoke pot, try the Pill, have a credit card in their own given names. Could have turned down the street preacher's tracts, set *Satan is Alive and Well on Planet Earth* back on the bookshelf and picked up *The Awakening* instead. Could have had a kind, firm stranger tell her *It wasn't your fault*. Or, thirty years later: could have listened when someone said *You should see someone about that [cough] [panic] [blooming edge of black on your finger]*. Could have looked from her back porch into the night sky choked with stars and asked, *Am I hearing what I think I'm hearing?* Could have known how it was all going to end, could have known that her own two hands held the rope. Could have relinquished her grip.

Could have called more often. Could have seen this coming. Could have intervened. Could have told her to knock it off, stand down, stop beating her own life to pieces on the rocks of anxiety and sorrow. Could it have been any better if I had said it more often? *Go for a walk. Go to church. Go to the shelter to volunteer. Go somewhere, anywhere that is not your own house and mind.* Could have wound back to the days before Katrina and said, *You won't make it so well on your own.* Could have stuck a therapist's number to her fridge before I shipped off to college. Could have bribed her somehow: *I'll come home twice a month if you go.* My own life could have been a bartering chip, a piece of currency, a minesweep. Couldn't it?

Could have been better at evoking a change, like the day that I told her to volunteer at a local dachshund rescue. She shrugged me off. *It'll make me too sad.* I was ready with the riposte: *It's a no-kill shelter, Mom.* She parried: *But there's nobody to take care of them all.* A thrust, a backwards leap: *That's why you volunteer. To help take care of them.* A jab, a slash, the finishing slice: *Well, I'll think about it.* A conversation ender, the open-ended promise that never comes to pass. How many times have I used it, too? And this was long before she totaled her car, before her borders had shrunk so dramatically. Even now, she's prodigious with fending off help. *Thanks so much for telling me I'm crazy! Boy, am I glad you called me today!* she says when I tell her to find a good therapist. Nevermind that she'll willingly offer, as casually as if pointing out a squirrel in her yard, *I'm sure I have PTSD.* So *could* remains a thought that hangs in the air, just out of reach and beautiful, like fireflies. Uncatchable *could.* Claustrophobic idea. A cage for a desperate mind.

Death, be not proud. Your work has been slipshod at best. She lit fire to her oxygen tube, and you still couldn't follow through. Couldn't take her with the car crash or sneak up when she's under the knife. Couldn't take her thirty-one years ago, when I, surprise child, split her belly like an overripe plum. Couldn't direct the blood clot you lodged in her finger to the cortex of her brain, or stop her heart with a merciful grip. She would say angels, of course, but what are you if not the blood-appeased specter of Egypt? Never has a woman been granted so many mercies. *New every morning*, she'd say, and she's right. We scramble around her with buckets. Each lintel she crosses glimmers crimson, and you, as always, pass over.

Darby means *free spirit.* My mother didn't know this when they named me; she chose it to honor the Irish side of her family. She didn't know, or forgot, that her family wasn't Irish, they were Scots: angry Presbyterians tight-lipped and laced up like a whalebone corset. Still, I feel that my name has given me power. *Free* like an ocean bereft of its moon. No continent or flag making *I* as much as the feel of my hand in the lake. Nothing left to inherit anyway except the nerve and the good sense to go when everything else has gone sideways. My mother always called me *bohemian,* and I wonder if that has borne out. I do not smudge her room with burning sage or press crystals to her skin. I do not make a vision board or send her self-help books. I make a logical argument for X. I show my work: numbers and facts laid out carefully for her to destroy. *I could have wished for more compassion,* she said. There's a heart in here all right, but it hangs from a ceiling, crystalline and jagged. A hardened and lengthening spur. A highland kind of heart, after all.

Desperate times call for all hands. My siblings and I hold conference calls when their children have been put to bed. We struggle to keep up with the crises: new carpet for the smoke-stained apartment, or a prescription that costs $800, or a vet bill that maxes her credit card. It gets worse over time. Social security won't cover her rent. The waitlists for vouchers are long. My brother starts covering bills. I send $100 and feel bad that I'm not sending more. Her apartment is riddled with ants, or fleas. She forgets her new phone in an Uber, and I locate the driver for her. She forgets her new phone in an Uber again, this time waits on a bench for an hour till the driver, unbidden, comes back. Every day, there's a new reason to worry she can't be left alone. But the smoke and the dog and the social worker says she's not incapacitated. So we link our fortunes together. We wring our hands and wait.

El Shaddai. Elohim. Elyon. The names of God are many, and from our mouths they pour *Not today* we say, or *take what you will so much is already missing* The baby tucks his bottom lip and chews She says *he's afraid of my face* or *we are going to see a real Harvest of family* The cards that do not come in the mail pile up *I am going to spend my weekend being a grandmother* My sister wraps the presents she buys herself and signs them *Love, Grammy*

Everything I've done has just been to keep her alive. I will—I must—fail. Before then, I do as much as I can. Fill out applications for Medicare, Medicaid, food stamps, free meals, free rides. We turn out our pockets and find faith struggling among the lint. Little trooper. Little traitor. Little bit of love choking on her admonishment: *I'm not a charity case.* We talk about moving her to Alabama, to North Carolina, to a place where her children can watch her more carefully. Nobody mentions California, where I live—too far away from everyone else. Too expensive, too strange for a woman who has lived in the South nearly all of her life. When my mother starts teaching a bible study at the senior center, the rest of the family relaxes: *What a community she's building,* they think. *Perhaps we should leave her in place.* I eye the curtains at stage left, expecting the swing of a pendulum axe. When my mother said *Maybe I'm here to redefine what can be done* I lost a breath I couldn't get back. Back home from rehab, she slept on the floor with her dogs. Their old bodies shuddered against hers as they inhaled   exhaled. The gap between what happens and what I imagine is full of the same old guilt. *You cannot keep her alive,* my husband says, sad-eyed. I know it but cannot believe. The gap between hope and what's hoped for widens at the river's mouth.

Echo chambers   the four of my heart: her blood, her bone marrow buried there. Lay our images one over the other and you will see   distortions   as if a mirror facing another, cracked through. What matches: eyes that shutter sight when what's disturbing looms   a willingness to lie to oneself, to lie to others about the self   a glass of Scotch where her Burgundy would be   and a voice behind blue light that croons *Everything is better alone   you're never free until you've given it all away*

Five: the number of children my mother carried in her body, protected with her own skin, fed with the current of her own blood. In the physical therapy rehab center, she loops the oxygen tube around her ears and fits the nose piece to her nostrils. *I smoked with all five of you*, she says, *and you turned out just fine.* The compressor gurgles. My sister and I trade looks, and I am grateful in that moment for our shared genes with all their buried ash. Outside this room, the nurses offer only praise. *We wish every patient was just like your mother. She blesses everyone she touches.* I wince, then wrench the grimace to a smile. There's no use disagreeing. The seer in sackcloth seems blindest of them all.

Forgiveness is supposed to be clean, but we know better. Always a sacrifice for moving on: a throat-slit kid, a spotless lamb. A long wandering that feels—and is—aimless. For years, my mother hid the fact of her first two children, her first marriage, and the reasons she abandoned them both. It wasn't until my sister was in high school that she stumbled by accident on the truth. How best to forgive a mother who hides so well from her own experience? And how to forgive a daughter who spins that life like a weaver at the loom, plaiting her weft through someone else's warp? For years, my mother's resentments—at terrible, low-paying jobs, at a husband too depressed to work, at bad credit and food stamps and the shame of such need out in public—grew as a gnarled vine. It took us a while to unspool it from our necks. Now, we know not whither we goest, only that the land on all sides is bad, and parched, and untamable except with a strike. We reconcile ourselves to our loss and we know: not everything will survive the whole journey.

Freedom is a curious drug for the compassless. Over time, my mother grew inward. Isolation as a choice, perhaps, or as a tongue pressing on the inner cheek's sore. Then Katrina happened, and the stories grew worse. *She fell asleep with a cigarette in her hand. She could not make it to the bathroom in time. She called me raging drunk again.* She dismissed a rattling cough as *a tickle in my throat.* She changed jobs and kept them for a while, but there was always someone who *just didn't like me,* or someone who *had to cut costs.* Some good reason for giving up, letting go, curling back into herself like the tendrils of a fern. Prayers, complaints, the bitter sound of *God knows what he's doing.* By the time she veered off the interstate into a guardrail, we all knew the cycle of crisis. We jumped, as always, at the sound of the crash.

God is a shape-shifter, a shade morphing in each believer's mind. In my mother's dreams, God takes the face of her father: stern jaw, eyes steel-blue like polished flint, mercy buried in his upraised palm. I watch her grasping against darkness and think, *Silence is evidence of nothing.* My mother buys a lottery ticket and requests a prayer from me. *If it is His will.* She offers to split the winnings. I say nothing. When she quit her Public Works job so many years ago, she felt that she had heard the voice of God, which said *No more working for corruptible men.* No need: consider the lilies of the field. In sleep my mother finds comfort in silence. The darkness then is a blanket, a blinder—a brief veil that hides the blinding light.

Good riddance, my mother thinks she'll say to this life. Trading up, you see. A world full of bloodied children and crooked, violent men for the gleaming streets of gold, the many mansions lined up in orderly rows, and a banqueting table full of good food and pitchers of wine. But I know the harder truth. She's never been more frightened. She's never felt so alone, nor heard so little in response to her prayers. I know this because the day the doctor examined her finger and said *We're going to have to amputate*, she trundled to the liquor store and bought the first cigarettes she would smoke since being admitted to the ER. *It was a little more than I could handle*, she said wryly, and what I heard was *Fuck it. I'm going to die in any case.* Her bible tells her that salvation can't be lost. The slate wiped clean ad infinitum. My mother folds into her body like a moth. There is no slate   no chalk.

Glass and light reveal inversions: image of a mottled pear behind the cup of water   stem stuck right while what I think of as *the real pear* leans to the left. How to know which one of these truths is ultimate? How to trust one's vision when illusions are as common as breath?   Is there only one pear truly   or has the bending light created two?   A pair of pears   A split truth shining and individual   Or else refraction uncovering the multiverse: one fruit goes left *and* right   In one small mottled moment   the body, full of potential   bearing infinite truths it will only surrender when pressed

Happiness:/ˈhapēnəs/ (n.) The state of being happy.

A worthless shit answer if ever there was one. And because the book won't tell us we look everywhere for a better definition. For years I squirreled cash in a black plastic pouch. For years I took every shift I could get, every job. Couldn't stop. My husband holds my face in his hands and consoles me: *The bottom is not going to drop out.* I chew my retort: *How do you know?* Poverty embeds in your bones. I remember how each time we moved, it felt like a long door was closing. I remember my brother's anger: he was making a bag of split-pea soup. The seething green mash filled the kitchen with its smell, and when he tried to serve it I cried. *There isn't anything else*, he snapped, and the sharp edge of his voice shut me up. I saw the lines of his worry as clear as sunlight through the trees. So I ate, like a good kid, for him. Now, silence no longer means goodness. Swallowing what's distasteful is no longer a virtuous act. *Forgive me*, I say as I dig at what seethes, what festers at the roots. If not happiness here, something at least akin to peace.

Her eyes were always my envy. How I wanted that blue for my own. Now, staring in the mirror, I think of what else I might have missed. What else I didn't. What lodges in the marrow, what unearths itself at night. A chest rising and falling with uneasy breath. A dream of many mansions, whether here on earth or otherwise. In our waking hours, we swell with buried stresses: her nose ballooning, my left eye puffing up. We do not dig at the root. We let ghosts make their homes in the moulding, unperturbed. Still, I've heard stories she's never told me. The husband who thought it was her fault. Two children standing naked in the yard, a concerned neighbor door-knocking her out of a haze. She looked her babies in the eye and she left them, and I worry that I understand how: connection felt as obligation, a binding that cries to be loosed. I only met them when they were grown—how long had it been since she'd seen them? Years after, they came to my wedding reception, a celebration held six months after my marriage to a man whose love for me is like a fathomless lake, a love that holds space for me as I am. My half-sister gave us an almond-shaped dish. My half-brother gave us some cash. We laughed and ate twice-baked potatoes. My mother fixed her grandson a plate. How strange, the ways our circles overlap. And can I be found in the gap? When my mother coughs, I feel the shudder vibrant in my chest.

Heat is a full-blown entity in the South, a respected foe for most of the year. And it became a character in my family stories, most of which involve a busted car in one way or another: *Summertime, I'm seven months pregnant and your father decides on a road trip. Fourteen hours in a car with no AC.* A mountain, a long day, a nauseated feeling that she now puts down to heat exhaustion, and the only available relief: Yankee tea, cold and dark and bitter. *And from that day*, she says, *I've always liked it better unsweet.* But I'm iffy on this version of things. Bitter has always been my mother's choice. Red ale, black coffee, the long recriminations that all point back to my father, or that terrible boss, or those who sat in the sanctuary taking communion and looking askance at her family—our querulous group, late each Sunday and never content with just listening. When the tiny cups of juice pass by, my mother sizes them up. Presented with sugar or wormwood, her inevitable choice will be gall.

It's summer in California, and the ships gleam as they slide toward the distant port and its rows of skeletal cranes. My lungs burn as I make my way down the runners' path on the beach. Next to me, a bike route winds in tandem and all kinds of people go by: rollerbladers in cutoffs, cyclists in padded shorts, tourists in four-person canopied carts that require synchronized pedaling. My mother got on an airplane today. It was a birthday gift from my sister. The device she carried on is a compact, flyable version of the long green tank my sister and I named *Marge*. A tiny streetsweeper drones by, kicks sand off the bike path and into my face. I splutter. I think of my mother, mask fitted to her nose and mouth in seat 30C. I press my hand into a side cramp and watch a pelican disappear beneath the ocean's surface, and for some reason, I think of the bald cypress, a tree that has learned how to breathe despite the marsh's best efforts to drown it. Adaptation: the best response to a hostile environment. I slow but do not stop.

In the space between what happens and what I see, there is an unfathomable deep I cannot cross. Cannot plumb. What it is like to live in her body, in her mind, what it is like to pray, to take an old sandwich from the microwave so the cold coffee can be warmed, I cannot possibly know. My heart breaks when she tells me she forgot the mozzarella cheese at the grocery store. She'd waited so long, spent almost all of her SNAP money, and forgot the crux of the casserole. Can't go back right away, can't afford a cab and definitely cannot drive. I know that this is not my cross to bear, but bear it I sometimes do. The odd chest-ache, the sigh. The sense of the body lying down, getting up, the shimmer of empty space around it.

Imagine one decision's difference: that first cigarette unlit. The first marriage put off for a Bachelor's degree. The boy and girl, tiny, not abandoned, not left behind so young they would have very few memories of her. Imagine ears to hear her sister, her doctor, her latter children, who flushed her cigarettes down the toilet. Imagine her son saying *You should stay for the retirement fund,* and imagine her listening for once. Or   imagine her in a walking group with other young moms, visor fitted to her sweating brow. Imagine her in a Junior League book club, reading *The Handmaid's Tale* with doctors' wives whose comfort she doesn't envy. Imagine her now like a department store ad, with a carefully sculpted white-haired bob, clip-on pearl earrings, a crisp collared shirt, and a wreath of smiling family members haloing her shoulders. A house clean and smelling like cinnamon. A catalogue table with catalogue crystal, a glinting set of napkin rings. Nativity set arranged just so: the holy mother surrounded, adored.

Judiciousness is a gentleman's trap, so I set myself up for the scandal. The problem's that my tongue will not cooperate. How do you tell someone, *Your standards of living are abysmal* or *You're killing yourself with neglect?* How do you say, *Stop making poor decisions in moments of great duress?* There's no handbook that can help me. This isn't your usual grief. I think of the ways my mother stood up for me when it mattered. How she pushed to get me braces and paid for them herself. How she took me on a college tour and prayed over my application. How she bought me a beaten-up car with money she didn't much have. She once felt pride in me when I acted like myself: stubborn, driven, single-minded. These traits now are a thorn in her side, and I wrestle myself over secrets. How much of this do I own? Can I claim the past from someone who will not face it? The tongue, uncooperative, will speak. The heart will cringe with the kind of guilt it's known for thirty-odd years and wonder: *What exactly is my ambition?*

Jesus looms large in every conversation. She works to understand him. *There's a lesson he wants me to learn*, she says, *and I'm trying to understand what it is.* I conceal a snort of derision, which isn't the fault of the Lord. The lessons seem pretty clear: quit smoking, put the seventeen-year-old dog with bladder cancer down, stop signing up for things you can't afford. But instead of any of this, I just say *Yeah*. My mother knows how her own mother died, in the spare room of a daughter's home, hooked up to oxygen and slipping more every day. I remember my grandmother's face, broad and kind and interested, framed with a short red bob and a clear plastic cannula. The cycle, it seems, is almost complete. But my mother pretends she's immortal. *He could still take me*, she says, *before things get that bad.*

Jesus loves me, or so the children's song argues. We don't talk very often, truth be told, and where this body goes does not concern me so much as the idea that the spirit might return: as junebug, as redfish, as a wild boar rooting through the swamp. There's no room in heaven for all of us, if the book's dimensions are to be believed. So send me back instead as something that's driven by instinct. Something that can't feel guilt or grief, disgust or a burning embarrassment. I'll gladly be the bobcat dulling its claws on a slash pine. I'll be the redwood standing anciently. The stingray sailing or reindeer grazing. Give me any body, cellulose or chitin or hide, but give me no more human mind.

Karma, though, at least in the Jain cosmology, has a physical presence and weight. Whether we're reborn as beast of the field, unfurling butterfly, or human sucking a world-changing thumb is determined by the drag of our past. When I do not call my mother back, or answer her text about earthquakes that happened hundreds of miles from me, how heavy do I grow? When she will not end the suffering of an animal, or tells her sister that nobody calls her, or lies about needing money for her prescriptions when what she really wants are cigarettes, how far down does the accreted karma pull her? Given another life, she'd like to be a sparrow, always under the watchful eye of God, or a white lily bowing in the breeze. Something simple, something from whom the Lord requires nothing. A pliant, forgotten blade on the hilltop where others have lain their burdens down.

Kindness, once virtue, now is an impediment: too much keeps our arms pinned to our sides. But what real alternative exists? She texts us one day to say that she's signed a new lease, and nobody responds for days. I know it's anger that stills us: we told her she needed to move, we told her she couldn't afford it. But for all she's lost, my mother has a grip on her agency. So what else can we do? We send her our money and we send her our kindness—good cheer, stifled complaints, this everlasting effort to spare her from herself. Each time, she finds new ways to make our kindness painful: racks up a rideshare tab, grumbles about the Senior Center's food, describes the birthday party my sister throws for her in North Carolina as *Several hours spent with multiple children under the age of 5*. Gives up, curls in, gnaws her own tail till she's in it up to her neck. Complains about the pain from her own clamped set of teeth.

Kant wrote, *I had to deny knowledge in order to make room for faith.* My mother ignores the note on the trailer. She ignores the pain in her blackening finger. She quits a job she can't afford to quit because she *never wants to work again,* but she says that the Lord has a plan. But there's cracks in that foundation. Years ago, when a drought hit her town, I heard an anger in her voice I hadn't heard before as she described some sparrows hopping in the yard, heads tipped back and beaks cracked open to the sky. She read this as a desperate thirst, and her anger at their pitiful dance found an unlikely home in God himself. *Why doesn't he do something about it?* she spat, her own mouth lined with dust. *Why will he not send the rain?* When her own diagnosis is grim, my mother will pretend that nothing is wrong. She will see the hand of God in a woman who tells her she made six figures blogging. She'll insist she can sell glass on eBay, or rent and drive a car for Uber, or become a home-care nurse. Her house will descend into filth. She'll go back to a full pack a day. She'll start to have trouble with eating, or more honestly, keeping the eaten food down. My sister will say it's a symptom of late-stage COPD. Nobody will tell that to my mother—no point. I'll think of the sparrows of summers ago, and wonder—all this space you made, all this room. Is your faith enough to fill it?

Lashes out when cornered, like a hit dog. Curses as if the sound could shove: *The house is in bumfuck Egypt*, she says when pressed. See, a friend from rehab offered her a room. Cheap rent. But my mother will not live under someone else's rules. As miserable as her lonesomeness is, it's a hard-won comfort to her. Nevermind that her children are squeezed to pay her bills. Nevermind that I'm suddenly thinking about American individualism in a new moral light. (*Is it cultural, this hesitation on my part to help her out?*) I spent so many years just barely getting by, and my mother sent help a couple of times. But it was money she should have been guarding: her inheritance, her FEMA money, the investments she long had cashed out. Had her generosity been short-sighted? Was I too selfish for taking it? We grit our way through assistance now, but I wonder: can a child's debt—for everything ever granted out of mercy or love—ever be fully repaid?

Love is an action, an active choice on another's behalf. Once upon a time, my mother loved me by letting me go. Would she have known how to ask me to stay? The day that I began the long drive from Slidell to Los Angeles, I handed her a photo as we were saying goodbye. In it, a tiny version of me squinted up at the camera and grinned. Long, messy, honey-colored hair swirled around my shoulders. I'd taken the photo for myself when I moved to college, before Katrina hit. The storm took everything that wasn't in a storage unit or in my mother's trunk and threw it in the marsh, erasing overnight great swaths of family memory. So I thought, of course, that she would like to have it. But I wasn't prepared for her grief. When I pressed the picture in her hand and said, *I wanted you to have this*, she clapped her free hand to her mouth and gagged. The sound that issued from her throat was animal—a doe keening over her fawn. An elephant circling the grave of its love. I panicked—what horrible thing had I done? I hugged her and patted her shoulders awkwardly, but she never really calmed. When I climbed into my car—the sun was getting higher, the road ahead was long—her face was still twisting with anguish.

Late July, two years after the accident: her 70th birthday. A milestone I wasn't sure she'd make. To celebrate   and for penance   I give her something she's always said she wanted: *A nice letter.* I fill it with truth, carefully, as one fills a beaker with what they hope is the correct ratio of fluids. Get it right and presto, gold! Wrong? An eyebrow charred off, a blistered lip. How to describe what my heart did when she said (after days of neglecting her mailbox) that the letter *just topped off my life*? I think about what that implies. A horizon spied. Seventy, I want to say, is so young. But as with all the other truths that will only upend equilibrium, I restrain it with the flat of my tongue. I write it down here. I remind her in writing that she showed me *what resolution looked like,* and I meant it when I said *I saw what your determination could do.* But the lament too is true, and even more so for glory now gone: a golden seashore eroded by inevitable storms. The spire of a shipwreck exposed.

My husband didn't meet my mother until we'd been married six months. This was not for lack of trying. We were supposed to spend one Christmas with her at my aunt and uncle's house. Mom, who still had a car and her relative health, planned to drive in from Houston. The short version of what happened is that my mother worried herself sick. The long version is: a week or so before our trip, a friend of hers lost a son, a Marine sergeant killed in Afghanistan. This upset my mother so much that the pain became a noxious, expulsive force she named *the stomach flu*. But stomach flus do not last a week. They do not fill your veins with lead, or turn your heart to dampened ash. I spoke to my mother in the week leading up to our flight. I cajoled her, urged her to go to a doctor, urged to her drink more water, assured her she'd be fine. I was sitting on the toilet when she called. It was 4:30 am on Christmas Eve and my now-husband and I were scrambling to get our things together so we could make it to the airport. I can still see the look on his face as he paused in the hallway, bags suspended in his hands. I can still hear the pathetic croak of her voice when she said, *Darby, I'm not going to make it.* So we spent our Christmas in the marshland, and my mother spent hers alone. That night, when a lightning storm shook the horizon in every direction but North, we stood on the porch, sweating beers clutched in our hands, and we watched.

My mother's mother dyed her hair red, owned an antique shop, and spotted planes in WWII. She found sobriety when my grandfather dragged her to AA. She planted a long bed of irises in Iowa and rode a mechanical chair up her staircase throughout her final, weakened years. We called her Grandma Cougar because that's what she drove: a forest green Mercury that sparkled in the Midwestern sun. Cougar shaped pottery with her hands and signed the bottom of a plate with a stick, the *y* of her real name cutting long and straight as an arrow. She tried to smoke her finger once—red glow of the pulse oximeter like a cigarette's tip. Did she regret laying my mother's birth certificate on the bed when she knew she was trying to elope? Or is that, too, a tall tale, a fabrication from my mother's revisionist history? Everything I would ask my grandmother now looms, a forest on the cusp of dark: a brimming silence before night creatures wake.

Marry me   Marry me   Merry me in faded photograph: toddler clad in buttercup yellow, bottom lip tucked in a crook-toothed grin. Or more serious me in a home video, shot at a snowy resort. Behind the camera my mother cajoles: *Darby, say something!* I look up and through the puffy red hood of my suit. I think for a moment. *God says   Be kind.* My mother laughs. *That's right,* she concedes. I look at her seriously. Always so serious, always so worried. (*Always the practical one,* she will huff twenty-seven years later.) I look into the lens and right at you and say, with all the gravity of a death-aware child: *But we can't say oh my god.* You can see me this concerned, of course—always uneasy and overworked, always inundated with the world's debris. But you cannot hear her voice, unburdened by longer years. You cannot see her as I saw her then, with beautiful dark hair that hung to her waist and a face less lined, more merry. The years have eaten the resort, the powdered hills, the cotton stuffing in the old red suit, but my mother and I are stuck on that mountain in time. She laughs again. I furrow the snow with the toe of my very small boot.

New Mexico, Summer 2014: my best friend and I are driving towards Albuquerque. As we cross under a bright yellow sign that says *Land of Enchantment* in desert red, we talk about family again. Her deadbeat father, my secret siblings. When I discovered them, an odd fantasy of mine came true: the revelation of relatives that I had never known existed. I hoped that they were rich. I imagined myself like a pauper child, rescued from the streets and admitted to a palace as its rightful prince. A poor kid's fantasy complicated by the scandal of my mother's hidden first marriage and the sudden epiphany that, holy shit, my parents had been people long before I ever was. Albuquerque: 140 and after a short pause I say, *Man, that was fucked up, huh?* My friend looks at me, and our laughter breaks into the car like a wave breaching a jetty. *That was really fucked up*, she confirms. *And you were always Little Miss Sunshine about it, which was kind of weird.* This is not as funny to me, I'll admit: that adaptability, that cheery acceptance of others' subterfuge. How clear it is now, the long, deep silences that bored their way between my own desires and the world. How many years I spent accepting others' problems before I finally learned to say *no*. How little I can tell her that still.

Not everything, of course, was disastrous. This explains the ache, the anger, the way my siblings and I can't always manage to be honest with her. She took joy in taking care of people once, like the time she brought a gallon of soup to my high school rehearsals when the whole cast of *Rumors* was sick. There were sunny days and trips to my aunt's house, trips to the antique show, trips to the deli for takeout. There was the old dog as a puppy—a surprise addition to the family, a creature she couldn't abandon. There was the sense of her blossoming post-divorce self, a confidence when she got a new job. Everything seemed possible then. How could I have understood the darkness underpinning it all? I was only one woman, and not even that: a child with an uninformed lens. Had I been able to see what was coming, I wouldn't have believed it just then.

November: the day after the election, my mother tells me that I should just give the man a chance. She says I'll be pleasantly surprised. I say, *I cannot talk about this right now*, and she says, *I do understand*. She does not. If the personal is political, then there's nothing I can argue to sway her that two divorces, five children, and a lifetime of working thankless jobs, sometimes several at a time, didn't manage. I wonder sometimes if my mother wonders how I happened. What road traveled from *God says be kind* to a sign with the word PUSSY in great glittering purple letters (an acrostic, no less)? How could she have produced this antithesis of the only advice she ever gave me, a refrain she'd chirp each time I left the house: *Be a lady!* The only time my mother ever marched was to protest *The Life of Brian*, a film she's never seen. Her picture made it into the local paper, apparently, and though I've never seen the clip, I know her hands gripped a sign that read *Boycott Blasphemy of our Lord*. If I could, I'd tell her something about this winding legacy of anger: her own and her father's. My father's. Me, a product of people for whom anger is another art. The quick snap. The long stew. The silent treatment tumbling into a blow up, the insults, the pitch of the voice that feels like a slap even if nothing else happens. *Why do you strive so hard against the truth?* I might ask. I imagine her shrug, her voice shrinking as her shoulders creep closer to her ears. *I don't know,* she might say. *Why do you?*

42

Ordering pizza even causes me grief. In high school, I moved in with her because I knew in the way that children know things about their parents that she needed me more than my father did. My brother says, *I acknowledge how difficult those years with Mom had to be*, but we had a good life for a while: an apartment all our own, a kind of freedom I hadn't enjoyed when the gloom of my parents' long civil war hung over the house. The apartment was bright and clean. She smoked, but outside. Sometimes, I parked my car in the grass by the floodwall and climbed up on the hood to watch sunlight dapple the lake. We ordered pizza once a week, and when I think about that time I do not feel like we suffered, except from the usual things: getting to work on time, finishing projects, paying bills, getting an A. The late-summer heat shifting coolly to fall and the future: college, Florida, heat and sun and forward motion. The days reel by like images from a film of someone else's life. We break from our old selves like icebergs shearing from a long white shelf. I float, I bob, I drift away. How blue I am; how clear, and how blue.

Only lonesomeness will do for the life my mother leads. But know this: she understands it does not have to be that way. Over and over again, she weighs her gains (someone to talk to, someone to share her food and her life with) against her losses (a critical voice that says *You can't just let your dog piss in this house* or *You cannot smoke in here* or *Can you clean this up please?*) My brother sends more money. I choke on my displeasure but he urges a *gentle conversation*. We clamber aboard the *Rota Fortunae*. It pulls us under, a crushing force, but we are patient for the pleasure of the apex, the good day, the victory that feels as if we have been rewarded for our righteousness. My mother lights another cigarette. The compressor gurgles. In Jainism, the wheel represents *ahimsa*, or the effort not to injure. Not to cause harm. My mother has never learned this and feels no pressure to be good. Her God is an awesome God, a purveyor of plagues and forgiveness. A cycle we learn to predict and a role we actively play. Ours is the hand of forgiveness. Hers is the hand that revolves the wheel, bringing good men to sorrow.

Other people do not understand. Who can blame them? Even my best friend cuts off my complaints with an admonishment: *Imagine if it was you.* I do imagine this, often. I am half her, after all, and where did she get it from, this need for the comforting cell of her solitude? My father once told me, *Your mother's dad really messed her up.* I've never quite learned what that means, though I've asked her about my grandfather's temper. She's told me about the traumas of war and the day he found his own father dead in the living room. Norman was only thirteen. My mother remembers one dinner—not the argument, but its climax—when Norman stabbed a pot roast and flung it at the wall. *I can still remember my mother,* she says. *She didn't even flinch.* O inheritance, O great laws of blood and property. What is mine is mine forever. What I do not wish to take, I cannot give away.

Poor choices. That is what the social worker calls it when we discover the oxygen tube. The carpet charred in a long curling line where the plastic flash-fired into the burls. The social worker explains why Medicaid will not yet cover a nursing home. She is not incapable, he says. Only full of *poor choices*: two pails full of Pall Mall boxes, an open can of dog food in the microwave, their feces in her closet. When they remove the tip of her ring finger, they will find E. coli in the bone. They will start an aggressive antibiotic regimen. I will find it hard to stay awake all week. This is the opposite of what I expect, but I let my body drag me away from the world. In sleep I do not see her. I dream, but nothing hurts.

Paul the disciple wasn't always Paul. Before his conversion, he was Saul of Tarsus, brutal and proud. His divine blinding was a mercy, a second chance bequeathed on a lonely stretch of road. After my mother careened off the interstate and into a guard rail, the hospital discovered that she was extremely hypoxic. The blue-tinted palms, the discomfiting cough. A future of tanks and inhalers. She said, *I never want to touch another cigarette again.* My brother assured us, *This time, it feels different.*

When my mother screams at my sister for insisting on truth a few months later, she does not hurl insults. She does not yell *You bitch* or *Fuck you* or *Go fuck yourself, you have no idea what this is like.* When my mother loses it and starts screaming at the top of her lungs, what comes through the phone is another attempt at guilt: *IT'S SCRIPTURE. BE YE KIND TO ONE ANOTHER. BE YE KIND. BE YE KIND. BE YE KIND.*

I imagine a thick pane of glass cracked straight through its middle. I imagine a lonely stretch of road. A smoking car. A hot blinding sun and no one, nothing around for miles.

Pain is a curious thing to inter in the plot of one's mind. It always comes roaring forth later, whether in nightmare or in the surprise snap: cat startled from sleep as my palm comes down on the table. Why I have kept these things for myself, I do not know. Confession is an act not just of truth-telling, but of laying one's burden down. How light my spirit would be if only I could unzip my chest, unlock the cage of sternum and ribs. But to what then would I cling, if the wind was the only thing left?

Roi, the French word for king, as in *Jesu, le roi du monde.* The stained glass window throws parti-colored light to the floor, and despite my knees on the padded rail, I'm not so sure I believe it. I write endlessly about dead toddlers, women struck by sarin gas, families drinking lead. I write but writing feels like sacrilege: the impotence of grief, of guilt. Everything else is in someone else's hands. So many evils in a given day— when will it be sufficient? My mother, of course, sees the hand of the Lord in the very world's spinning   believes that the sparrows, the prisoners dangling from trees, the migrants lost to the maw of the sea remain under the divine Eye   *I just thank Jesus,* she says, when my brother sends her money   or my sister buys her a plane ticket   or I sign her up for healthcare   or the apartment decides not to evict her because her sister forks over money   and I admit to covetousness: I want this praise for myself   I want to cede everything to the Lord's hands, but it turns out   that the king has gone mad or gone fishing, or else let the world fall to His jesters   and the yoke left uncarried will rot   and the white lily crumple beside it

Root   or, more accurately, radicle: *the first part of a seedling to emerge during the process of germination*. Emissary. Scout. Believer that brings back water so the stem can nose through loam, can spread its leaves and photosynthesize. There are two kinds of radicles, it turns out   the kind that grow back toward the seed casing, for what purpose the book doesn't say   and the kind that grow away   putting space and silicate between itself and home.   Darwin said that the radicle acted like *the brain of one of the lower animals*   just a sensory processor, like the spiked arms of a jellyfish   or whatever propels the gormless sea cucumber   But that which strikes out and leaves to do the dirty work knows that the home case soon will split   and the ascendant stem, the spreading roots   will outgrow what provided them shelter

Realism is not my mother's strong suit. She flatly refuses when I tell her that death would be mercy for the dog, despite his bladder cancer and his paralyzed back. When I see her that summer of her car accident, of her diagnosis, of her long stint in physical therapy to regain the use of her lungs, we will go to the vet to visit him. The dog will lick my ankle weakly. I'll pat his thin, gray head and feel a kind of sorrow that I'll try to describe over and over again but cannot. Little sad symbol of decline. Little emperor brought low by time and illness. Sometimes, I can't blame her for wanting to keep her companion, but I will remember the way he shook as he dragged himself across the linoleum. I will remember the antiseptic smell of the room, and my mother's blackened ring finger as she held him and cooed. The air in the room will be woolen, and I'll know I won't see him again. My mother will close her eyes and kiss the dog's gray ear.

Sin is pleasurable only for a season, but the length of the season can vary. My mother has smoked for fifty years. Going on fifty-one. She knows that the Pall Malls will kill her, but this isn't what's frightening to her. My mother wants to die. But as with everything, she wants it in a very particular way: nighttime, a dog curled beside her sleeping body, her chest rising as breath fills then exits her lungs. Then, suddenly, the great bellows of her heart gives out, deflates. She never sees it coming. The dream she's dreaming continues, expands, fills with light. There is the robed figure with the outstretched arms. There are the seraphim circling the throne. The blink of an eye without the eye. The body, left behind, unremembered.

Sand in my teeth: the feeling of calling her bluff. I say, *You're going to hate me, but*—and she rushes in: *Oh, I do! I do hate you.* Maybe it's just a joke, like it was a joke to preface my own point in this way, but something in me knows it's a little bit true. I am a burr buried in my mother's flesh, always willing to say what she'll despise. But what she doesn't know: where she sees an uncharitable secularist, someone who's forgotten mercy and grace, I see myself at six or seven, hiding in the closet. I'd taken my sister's chewing gum—only one pink shred of Big League Chew, but she told. I denied everything. My mother pulled the wooden spoon from her purse, explained calmly why this would happen: *not the stealing, but the lying.* I spit as I run down the beach path, remembering. How could a child raised at her knee ever learn that lying is wrong? How can a child full-grown, reeling from her mother's lies—that nobody ever calls her (they do), that she was let go in a layoff (she was fired for skipping her shifts), that she's out of money and needs her prescriptions (out of money, yes; by prescriptions, she means more cigarettes)—bear to be pleasant? My friend's admonishment rings in my ears: *Imagine if it was you.* My sides burn with anger and the breath that my lungs fight to keep. *I will not,* I tell myself, grunting. *I will not allow that to happen.*

Satan was an outsized villain in my early life. Even before I was acquainted with my mother's apocalyptic literature, I was initiated in the spiritual battle. I wailed with terror when my sister told me, *Hell's so hot your skin will melt off.* She regrets this now, of course, but I flung myself on my bed and I begged: *Please please please don't send me to hell   I'll do anything you want, I promise   I'll be good, I promise.* My mother insisted that Satan wasn't a horn-headed, raw-skinned devil—he was worse. He was a beautiful but monstrous deceiver, a silken Deluder sowing damnation with honeyed lies about the superiority of creation to Creator. For years, I pledged to the Christian flag and sang *Onward, Christian Soldiers.* Now, I know that we don't need a revolutionary clothed as a snake to tempt us into evil. We don't need a third-party villain to plot our grand destruction. Clever, tool-wielding animals, we've figured it out on our own.

Terrible is the punishment of the Lord for those who believe in such things. My mother believes in the rapture, and for this reason, she says, she will not donate her organs. She says in the end times, everything will be called back to its original place—even if borrowed, even if embodied in somebody else. *I wouldn't want someone to be driving along,* she says, *and POOF—their heart, my heart, is suddenly missing.* As absurd as the logic may be, I admit that I admire her concern. Forget for a moment that nobody wants her porous lungs. Nobody wants her congested heart, or the liver run through a lifetime of bottom-shelf Burgundy. What an odd sort of way for the Lord to proceed: hearts and livers and kidneys reclaimed, reassembled. What if the body is buried for years, and the soft tissue is processed through the bellies of worms, and the worms get eaten by robins, and the robins get eaten by hawks? Or, if a dead sinner's heart is placed gently in the believer's chest, will there be a palpating muscle left in the La-Z-Boy when the rest of the body is taken? There are so many questions my head is the head of a pin   and innumerable angels rattle within.

Tipping a vase, my mother would inspect its bottom: *Fenton. Cambridge. McCoy.* Names scrawled, pressed, or stuck where they were least intrusive. She got good at spotting a gem, and I, her constant companion, learned too: *flame crest. hobnail. epergne.* The lush opacity of milk glass or paper-thin green of Depression. This was an extension of her own mother, who got into antiquing later in life. I wonder now if this was another way to find her, buried not in a family grave in Massachusetts but in the shelves of Westmoreland and Steuben. Her laugh released from a hand-painted atomizer. Her interests and tastes kept in a footed compote. But this was only part of it, after all. It was the dream of the internet, too, the eBay buzz of chat rooms and auctions and a community that called themselves *Glassies*. It was meet-ups and conventions, it was a digital camera that my father resented (*Squandering your money,* he scoffed)—the first that a novice could buy. I remember the charm and the gloom of antique malls. But mostly, digging through the old box of my brain, I remember: a true kind of happiness in her. How far away it seems now, but how real. Trapped in time, as an ancient ewer submerged in the old city's ruins.

Tell me: what should I do? I met a woman once who gave her mother a kidney. They were a perfect match and when I said *Wow, how wonderful of you*, she just shrugged and said, *Well, you know, you only get one mother.* Years ago, mine cashed out her savings and bought gold bars because she didn't trust the government. A month before my wedding reception—and two months before the accident that would total her car and land her in the hospital where all the long-ignored truths would come out—she quit another job. Her plan was to make money by selling some hand-painted glass. Then my aunt, a nurse, took a drop of her blood, and the results weren't good: those blue-tinged palms were indeed out of breath. But my mother wouldn't go to a doctor because *I don't want it to be all about me* when the big party was coming up, the party for her daughter and the son-in-law she hadn't yet met. No matter how I begged I could not make her go. So I let myself do what all brides do—I put myself first for a change. I pulled her on the dance floor just once, my bare feet on the cool Carolina grass, her favorite song coming over the speakers. She'd been singing it the day before, all wrong: *Uptown funky whoa. Uptown funky whoa.* But under the soft yellow glow of the string lights, she looked a little pained, like she was concentrating hard. I should have known what was happening, but I didn't. I put myself first. I put out my arm to stop her when she turned to leave. *Just this one dance,* I begged. *I can't,* she said. *Come on, please,* I said, trying to sound upbeat. *You don't understand,* she started to say, but a friend who must have seen what was happening appeared unexpectedly, shouting *Dance circle!* The crowd gathered quick. My mother, trapped, gave in. Turned her eyes to the sky and kept them fixed on what I don't know as she marched softly in place, hips swaying as little as possible. When the music faded out, she let me hug her before she padded off.

Verily, begins the tale: a statement of truth from the start. I make no claims to gospel. Can only do impression. My mother is hard to transcribe, like a moth that turns to smoke when you cup it in your hands. Once, she went to the senior center for bingo, a game she derides as boring (*For old people, but it's something to do*). Sat next to a woman who only spoke Spanish, and who had never played bingo before. Exasperated, my mother explained on the phone: *I did my best to help her. Kept looking at her card and pointing to numbers she had. She just frowned at me, mostly. Couldn't understand a lick of English.* I laughed silently into my sleeve. Of course the woman who refers to immigrants as *illegals* would find herself trying to help when the idea from her TV was real, was a person. Same woman who taught a remedial math class of misfits, who dubbed an angsty goth teen *my little Satanist* and gave him lunch money when he was hungry. Of course she assumed she had something to say, and it was the recipient who fell short on the transfer. Same person who, as a grocery demo worker, didn't understand why Muslim families didn't want to eat samples with pork. When I was a child, and sick, she would stroke my head till I slept. Since I moved to California—*a socialist state*—she's never once come to visit. We think of truth as a fixed point, or as a tower that brick by brick takes form. But it's the sea: all roil and foam. Part calcite, part cartilage. An unfixed shape with an unfixed temperament. A place of origination, all-encompassing. Never a place of finality, until yours are the bones in the wreck.

Voices float home from the ages. I can hear my grandfather's yell and the sound of the pot roast hitting the wall. My grandmother's silence balloons. My mother's young face still is shifting: is she angry? Upset? *We never talked about it,* she will say. The legacy of our mothers runs deep. My bones hum with their sorrows. My skin sings with their triumphs: a habit kicked, or children raised. I fold in and look further for Gertrude, who had a tubercular hip and a custom-made shoe to even her stride. Massachusetts newspaper clippings don't mention what she did in her free time, or whether she kept lovers once her husband had died. They don't tell me the names of the women before her, nor the names of her pets, if she had them. Just a surname, a marriage, a slate of six kids. Of Cougar, I know more: *She buried two husbands and had a boyfriend when she died,* as my aunt likes to remind me. Of my mother, even more: she was, for a time, a synchronized swimmer. She once owned a raccoon named Sharon, and an armadillo who dug at the linoleum. Her father was disappointed when she wasn't a boy. She approached my father first—knocked on his door with a fresh cup of coffee. Her daring, her courage, her flirtation: I hold these too in my palms. I am, after all, of her line. The blood that rang in her reverberates through me.

Vernal, this song in my head. This green in the post-winter lawn. What is it with poets and spring? The answer, as usual, is death. We are not blind to the cycle of things. When geese return over the southern hills, the whole world joins them in facing the sun. Once upon a time, my mother was good with her hands: she cut figurines with a bandsaw and painted them. She cross-stitched bible verses to hang on the wall, and a goofy-looking sea monster running into a ship—a present for my father, Navy Commander, when her love for him wasn't yet spoiled. Was her solstice the day she dressed up in a sari to teach the children in church about missionaries? Was it the year she received her inheritance? Was it the day that she signed the divorce papers, or the day that she signed for the five-bedroom house and carried me around on her hip? Whatever the zenith, it's passed. The geese have turned back. The chill has crept back in the air. The long winter stretches before us, and we prepare ourselves as best as we can.

Winding red clay   Mississippi mud staining my hands murderous. Three years old painting my nails with something that peels off easy. Paint, peel. Paint, peel. Whippoorwill trilling somewhere beyond the fence. Bald old snake in the underbrush, waiting: thin nose-slits catching the scent of disaster. Behind the house, a greenhouse. The collie, bursting with instinct, retreated there to whelp. O the days of blood unbothersome. The puppies tiny, slick with their mother's interior—or was that the sheen of summer, the shimmering days of harvest moon and the perfect globes of muscadine grapes? Did the fever dream begin or end with mottled beans in my mother's palm? Everything began, but not yet. There was still a pregnant moment. A capsule of time that soon, I could not have known, would burst.

Why snakes get branded evil. My childhood riddled with them: cotton-mouths and copperheads, and the thin, bright green grass snake flailing as my sister ran, yelling *Look what I caught!* It's us who should be condemned: grass snake's green smeared with red dribbling from its slack little mouth. Or the one that got caught in my mother's mercy—she ran it over in our behemoth old car, a puce Plymouth we christened Large Marge, and not wanting to prolong its misery, backed up and tried it again and again, peeled out, even, until it managed to limp off despite her. The spade my father brought down on the neck of a thick black king snake, a true name if ever there was one. The heat, the scent of the clay. The scent of fallen pecans rotting at the back of the property. The head severed at last, my father came inside for iced tea.

Wail and shake those chains all you want, the voice in my head insists: you'll never get the bayou back. Never walk the block, that exact one-mile circle under pine trees, again. How many days we've lost to the tide turned rebel come up to swallow the whole thing, frame, foundation, windows and all. Wilt, summer squash, and writhe, summer snake. There are memories buried here no spade can excavate. No polished tomb can name. It's difficult to show you how still, how heavy that air can be. It's difficult to tell you about the drooping pestilent moss, or the bobcats caterwauling in the marsh, or the way I hung over the water for hours with a packet of bread and a fishhook and counted the perch I reeled in: 33. I stopped at Jesus's number. The perch, numb-lipped, returned each time I threw them back, each time the hook plashed down. Bread. Copper-colored water and who knows what lurks beneath. I do: the gar with his long, warped snout. The alligator in ancient wise armor, his tail that can break millennia. The crab that knows the upside of decay, and the flounder keeping both eyes on us all. The great blue heron turns his gaze toward the lake. I turn the lens back to myself.

Your MOTHER Was Pro-Life! proclaims the bumper of a car in front of me. I can't escape: L.A. traffic on a workday afternoon. So I argue with it instead. My mother was a good mother, I say, many years ago. But from the vantage point of adulthood, I see the things she gave me: anxiety, self-centeredness, a fear of death that threatens to keep me off airplanes. O yes, she is pro-life, but I suspect it's because she doesn't really believe in anything else. Witness her timorous hope that she'll be raptured before she can die. Her long-neglected body swept up in the light, made whole. She of the blood affliction, she of the truncated hand reaching and reaching and never quite brushing the hem.

Years from now, or maybe not, I might have my own children, too. What will I do? Will I hand them this and say, *It's a long story without a whole truth, but you should know it all the same?* When I picture myself with an infant, I feel terror disguised as disinterest. This need to be insulated, this desire to never be needed—what could survive in my orbit? *You just want to be left alone,* my husband says. My mother curls up in her chair. She makes a nest out of blankets for the dog who survives. She makes too much casserole and watches old game shows on an iPad that somebody bought her. These comforts are not really comfort, but I wonder if somehow she's happy. *If I die alone,* she said. The sentiment sounded sincere.

You may be hoping this will end on a positive note, or that there's a grand lesson I've learned, some wisdom to impart. I will tell you this: I am enjoying a cold iced tea, unsweet, just the way my mother drinks it. She is alive, possibly arguing with a taxi driver or watching TV with the volume too loud while she smokes and surfs the web. I sort chunks of the past and present and attempt to form a whole picture. Most days I feel numb, but there's always a low-simmering grief. We've spoken, but there is much I haven't said all these years. When she passes on to whatever awaits us (I pray for her satisfaction), I will know that there are thousands of things I never said to her. (Unless by chance she reads this, and in the reading, what new blade-edge will sever the threads that connect us?) Our lives will be two separate islands which only a vast ocean connects. I feel the pain of this long before it happens, but I do not believe I can change it. *I could have wished for more compassion*, she said. My heart is a sieve through which my grief and love, my anger and desperation leak unending. Thousands of miles away, she raises the thumb of her uninjured hand. Quick *shk!* and a flame appears. My mother is illuminated for the briefest span of time.

ACKNOWLEDGMENTS

Thank you to Diane Goettel and the rest of the team at Black Lawrence Press for making this book a reality. Your passion, care, and talents have made this process a dream.

I am also grateful to the editors of *RHINO 19*, where *[Marry me]* and *[Wail and shake those chains]* first appeared.

Special thanks to Eric Pankey for all of the encouragement and faith over the years, and for being one of this book's earliest, most important readers.

To all the good friends and fellow travelers who have influenced me as a thinker, writer, teacher, and artist: thank you for sharing your light. Thanks to Michele and RJ for their early readings and invaluable feedback. And Alyse Knorr: thank you for remembering the dachshunds. I'm so grateful for your friendship and your encouragement to send my work out again.

Cassia, thank you for all the long conversations and the bottomless well of your love. You have a lion's heart. Daniel, thank you for your steadiness and kindness, and for always encouraging my better angels. I admire you both to the ends of the earth. Dad: thank you for teaching me to dream big and unabashedly, and for my favorite advice of all time: *Sometimes, you gotta get mean.* I love you. Stephanie, Ashley, and Leeann: you are my sisters, too. Thanks for always being a part of my story.

To Wren, who was only an idea when I first began this book: loving you is the greatest privilege. Thank you for letting me take care of you.

And to Spencer, who is the wisest, sharpest reader I know. This book would not exist without you, your support, and your gentle encouragement to let the love in, too. Thank you for your love and for making this, and me, better and stronger through it all. *Bohfron*.

Finally, for Mom: this book would not exist without you for a thousand different reasons. Thank you for teaching me not just how to read, but how to love and respect both the magic and the terrible power of language.

You used to like to reference an old song—the sheet music for which you picked up at an antique mall—as a joke. "You'll never miss your mother till she's gone!" you would say in a sing-song voice, usually when you knew we were frustrated. I never knew how to tell you that that wasn't true. That I missed you all the time.

I love you.

REFERENCES

A Note on the Text:

The form for this book was inspired by Lamentations 3, which was, in the original Hebrew, written in abecedarian tercets. Lamentations 3 has 66 lines, so this book has 66 prose poems, the first three of which begin with "A," the next three of which begin with "B," and so on. The Hebrew and Latin alphabets are not directly equivalent to each other (and I am neither a scholar nor a speaker of Hebrew, ancient or otherwise), so while the number of pieces in All the Lands We Inherit *is faithful to the number of lines in the original poem, I took liberties with the specific letters I decided to use (for example, the letter J, which has no counterpart in Hebrew).*

Where these poems allude to biblical texts, I have borrowed the language of the King James Bible—the translation my mother preferred.

References

3: "as Hawthorne says" references the last line of Nathaniel Hawthorne's *The Scarlet Letter*: "Be true! Be true! Be true! Show freely to the world, if not your worst, yet some trait whereby the worst may be inferred."

4: "Send me off on an ice floe" is a reference to the disputed practice of senicide in some indigenous communities of the Arctic.

6: "Birthright not as lands and blessings" is a nod to the story of Esau. See Genesis 25 and 27.

7: *Satan is Alive and Well on Planet Earth* (1972) is one of several works by the dispensationalist Christian writer, Hal Lindsey. *The Awakening* (1899) is a feminist novel by Kate Chopin.

10: "Death, be not proud" references John Donne's Holy Sonnet 10; "the blood-appeased specter of Egypt" and the "lintels glimmering with blood" is a reference to the Angel of Death in Exodus 12:23; "New every morning" is from Lamentations 3:22-23.

14: "hope and what's hoped for" is an allusion to Hebrews 11:1: "Now faith is the substance of things hoped for, the evidence of things not seen."

16: The "seer in sackcloth" references Tiresias, the blind prophet who tells Oedipus the truth ("I say that you yourself are the very man you're looking for": Sophocles, *Oedipus the King*, lines 410-11). Oedipus suggests that his blindness is a reason not to trust him.

17: "we know not whither we goest" is a play on John 14:5 ("Thomas saith unto him, Lord, we know not whither thou goest; and how can we know the way?"); "untameable except for a strike" is an allusion to Numbers 20:2-13.

19: "Consider the lilies of the field" comes from Matthew 6:28.

20: The description of "streets of gold" comes from Revelation 21:21; "many mansions" is lifted from John 14:2; and the "banqueting table" comes from Song of Solomon 2:4.

26: "my cross to bear" is an allusion to Luke 9:23 ("And he said to them all, If any man will come after me, let him deny himself, and take up his cross daily, and follow me.")

28: "a thorn in her side" is an allusion to 2 Corinthians 12:7 ("And lest I should be exalted above measure through the abundance of the revelations, there was given to me a thorn in the flesh, the messenger of Satan to buffet me, lest I should be exalted above measure.")

29: "He could still take me": for more on the Rapture, see 1 Thessalonians 4:15-17.

30: "the children's song" is a reference to "Jesus Loves Me," a popular children's hymn by Anna Bartlett Warner (1859); "if the book's dimensions are to be believed" is a reference to Revelation 21:16, which supplies measurements for the post-apocalyptic city of New Jerusalem.

31: "a sparrow... under the watchful eye" is a reference to "His Eye is on the Sparrow," a hymn by Civilla D. Martin (1905); "where others have lain their burdens down" is an allusion to Matthew 11:28. ("Come unto me, all ye that labour and are heavy laden, and I will give you rest.")

33: The Kant quote is from his essay, "Critique of Pure Reason."

44: "Her God is an awesome God" is an allusion to the contemporary hymn, "Our God is an Awesome God," by Rich Mullins (1988).

47: The story of Paul's conversion on the Road to Damascus can be found in Acts 9. "Be ye kind to one another" comes from Ephesians 4:32 ("And be ye kind one to another, tenderhearted, forgiving one another, even as God for Christ's sake hath forgiven you"), the authorship of which is attributed to Paul.

49: "Jesu, le roi du monde" comes from the St. Louis Cathedral in New Orleans. "So many evils in a given day" is an allusion to Matthew 6:34

("Take therefore no thought for the morrow: for the morrow shall take thought for the things of itself. Sufficient unto the day is the evil thereof"); "the yoke left uncarried" borrows the language of Matthew 11:29. ("Take my yoke upon you, and learn of me; for I am meek and lowly in heart: and ye shall find rest unto your souls.")

50: All information about the radicle, including the Darwin quote, comes from Wikipedia.

52: "sin is pleasurable only for a season" is best attributed to Hebrews 11:25. ("Choosing rather to suffer affliction with the people of God, than to enjoy the pleasures of sin for a season.")

54: "Onward, Christian Soldiers" is a hymn with lyrics by Sabine Baring-Gould (1865) and music by Arthur Sullivan (1871).

55: The question of how many angels can dance on the head of a pin first appears in William Sclater's 1619 work, *An exposition with notes upon the first Epistle to the Thessalonians*. It is also credited to William Chillingworth's *Religion of Protestants* (1639). In both cases, it is a derisive allusion to St. Thomas Aquinas's *Summa Theologica*.

64: "She of the blood affliction" is a reference to Luke 8, Matthew 9, and Mark 5.

Kristine Boel

DARBY PRICE was born and raised in Southeast Louisiana. She earned her BA at Florida State University and her MFA at George Mason University, where she was a Heritage Fellow and the Poetry Editor for Phoebe. Her work has appeared in *Cimarron Review*, *Beloit Poetry Journal*, *RHINO*, *Redivider*, and *Zócalo Public Square*, among others, and her reviews and interviews have appeared in *The Collagist* (now *The Rupture*) and *The Southeast Review*. *All the Lands We Inherit* is her first full-length collection.